Charles Danso

Daddy, Let Go of My Hand

Charles Danso

DADDY, LET GO OF MY HAND

LESSONS FROM UPBRINGING WHILE FORGING NEW ONES

CHARLES DANSO

Charles Danso

Daddy, Let Go of My Hand

Charles Danso

Dear Reader,

Thank you for taking the time to read Daddy, Let Go of My Hand. This book is deeply personal to me and sharing it with you has been both humbling and rewarding. It is my hope that the stories and reflections resonated with you, offering guidance, inspiration, or simply a moment of connection on your own journey.

If this book has touched you in any way, if it made you reflect, smile, or see parenting in a new light, I would appreciate it if you could take a few moments to share your thoughts in an honest review on Amazon or other sources.

Your feedback not only helps me as a writer but also allows other readers to discover this book and decide if it might be the right fit for them. Whether your review is just a few sentences or a detailed reflection, your voice matters, and it would mean the world to me.

With gratitude,

Charles Danso

Daddy, Let Go of My Hand

I dedicate this book to my wife Edwina, children Zylo and Zander, whose love and support have been my foundation and strength.

To all whose life journey I have been privileged to cross paths with. You have given purpose to write this book.

Thank you.

Charles Danso

Praises for Daddy, Let Go of My Hand

"A beautifully written, profoundly moving reflection on the delicate balance between holding on and letting go as a parent. A must-read for anyone navigating the journey of parenthood."

"Charles Danso captures the essence of parenting with grace, empathy, and wisdom. This book is a gift to anyone seeking to build stronger, more meaningful relationships with their children.

*****

Introduction

Parenting is one of life's most profound journeys, a delicate dance between guiding a child through life's uncertainties and stepping back to let them discover their path. *Daddy, Let Go of My Hand* is a heartfelt exploration of this journey, offering reflections on the bittersweet transition from dependence to independence. Through deep personal anecdotes, thoughtful observations, and timeless lessons, this book delves into what it means to be a present and intentional parent.

At its core, this book is a tribute to the courage it takes to let go, not out of indifference, but out of love. It celebrates the quiet moments of connection, the hard lessons learned, and the unshakable bond between a parent and child. It examines the role of a father not just as a provider but as a mentor, a protector, and a cheerleader standing proudly on the sidelines as their child takes flight.

This is not a guidebook filled with rigid rules. Instead, it is an invitation to reflect on the universal joys and challenges of raising children, from the sleepless nights of infancy to the poignant moments of watching them step into the world on their own. It acknowledges the doubts and fears parents carry, as well as the immense pride that comes with witnessing a child's growth.

Daddy, Let Go of My Hand is for every parent striving to leave a legacy of love, resilience, and independence. It is a testament to the enduring power of presence and the quiet strength required to prepare children not just to survive but to thrive.

Daddy, Let Go of My Hand

As you turn these pages, may, you find inspiration, solace, and the courage to embrace the journey of letting go, knowing that every step forward is a testament to the foundation of love you have built. This is not just a story about parenting, it is a story about life, love, and the unending gift of believing in one another.

Charles Danso

ALSO, BY CHARLES DANSO

Blueprint Values for Success

Table of Contents

Chapter One

Roots and Bonds

To newer generations in the United States of America, the words "father" and "daddy" are as different as night and day. One is just a title, a formality, almost sterile in its form, while the other held warmth and familiarity, a safety blanket that wrapped around a person's very existence. These two words are never to be confused. From generation X to the latest generation, it is learned that a father could create a child, but it was a daddy who raised one.

In a world where labels are often tossed around loosely, "father" and "daddy" represent entirely different beings. A father is simply a man who, through biology, contributes to a child's creation. His role, though critical in a physical sense, often ends there. He might hold pride in the knowledge that his lineage continues, that his genetic footprint is embedded in the world, but it is a passive pride, one unaccompanied by the sacrifices or sweat it takes to nurture a child. In contrast, a daddy is an active participant in his child's life. He is there in everydayness, in the grit and grind that defines parenthood. He is the one who rises before dawn to provide, protect, and be present.

He knows he does not have to be there every day. He chooses to be. He gets up each morning with a purpose that extended beyond himself. He provides, he saves, he worries about his child's future, all with a steadfastness that can be recognized as pure, selfless love. He sacrifices because he wants their life to be better than his own. He made me feel safe in ways words could never truly describe. He showed up when it mattered most, not because he had to, but because he wanted to.

Daddy, Let Go of My Hand

A daddy understands that he is his child's first real-life friend, their first hero, and the first person they look up to. It is a role he carries like armor, knowing that he is a role model not only by intention but by mere existence. He wears the weight of responsibility with a quiet dignity, and though he knows that his child's friendship is a privilege, he also realizes that it is not his duty to be liked. Instead, his responsibility is to be a teacher, a guide, and a protector. Daddies know this. He has a tough love streak, but it is rooted in his understanding that life would not always be kind, and he wants them prepared.

Through him, they learn that discipline is not about control, but about love. When he teaches them the value of hard work, it is not to make their life harder but to instill resilience. They may not understand it at the time, because it often feels like a harsh lesson. But as they grow older, they will see the value in these early teachings. They will see how, like a blacksmith molding metal, he is shaping them into someone who can withstand life's inevitable trials.

Being a daddy often means sacrificing personal desires and dreams for the sake of one's children. It is about putting someone else's needs above your own without resentment, understanding that in giving so much, you are not losing anything, you are gaining the pride of watching your child grow strong, kind, and capable. Daddies do not talk about sacrifice, and he does not have to. His actions speak louder than any words can. Many times, when he comes home, exhausted from work, he will still make time to listen to his child's stories, ask about their day, or help them with homework. He will often be tired, yet never too tired for them.

For a daddy, the role of protector is a natural extension of his love. Daddies teach their child that he will do anything to keep them safe, that their

Daddy, Let Go of My Hand

well-being is his top priority. It is not just about physical safety; it is about making sure they feel secure in every sense of the word. He is the steady hand that guides them, the voice that reassures them, the presence that grounds them. They know, without question, that he will face any challenge, take on any hardship, for their sake.

One of the hardest lessons he must learn and, in turn, teach them, is the balance between being a friend and being a guardian. He wants to be both, but he understands that sometimes, to guide them effectively, he cannot always be a friend. There will be times when his decisions may seem strict, his expectations high, and his patience thin. He knows that there will be moments when they will not understand his choices, times when they would feel resentment or frustration. But he also knows that his role is not to constantly seek their approval but to ensure their growth. He often takes on the burden of being the "bad guy" when necessary because he knows that the lessons they learn will serve then far beyond those moments of conflict.

One day when they look back, they will realize that he did not do it for accolades, for recognition, or for gratitude. He did it because he loves them deeply. He did it because he knows that if he does not set the foundation, life's inevitable struggles will be harder for them to bear. And in his quiet way, he teaches them that true love is often tough, sometimes unappreciated in the moment, but unyielding and enduring.

A daddy, unlike a father, will not hesitate to give his life for his child's. He may never need to face that choice, but in his heart, he has already decided. He will do it without a second thought, not as a grand gesture but as the ultimate act of love. He is the one who will walk through fire, stand up against any threat, face any fear, all for the sake of his child's safety and happiness, just like a true mom would.

Daddy, Let Go of My Hand

And as they grow older, they will start to see the toll it takes on him. The late nights, the endless worries, the sacrifices he makes without ever asking for anything in return. They will realize that his strength is not just in his ability to be there physically but in the way he supports them emotionally. He teaches them what it means to love deeply and to give without expecting anything back. He shows them that being a parent is not about titles or biology; it is about choice, action, and unbreakable commitment.

In a way, a dad does not only raise his child; he shapes them. He teaches them that love is not about what you get, but about what you give. And in doing so, he will leave an indelible mark on their soul, one that they can carry with them every day. They will know that, in his eyes, his duty is never truly completed. He would always be there, ready to step in if they needed him. And that is the difference, a father might see his duty as done, but a daddy knows that his love, his guidance, and his role are forever entwined with his child's life.

As they look back on those early years, they may see the subtle, often unspoken bond that formed between them, shaped by his love, his sacrifices, and his willingness to do whatever it takes to give them a strong foundation. He is more than just a father; he is a daddy. And that made all the difference.

Everything you have read up until this point is not from my experience growing up, but rather what I am trying to create with my own children. This ideal of a daddy, present, dedicated, and selfless is a vision that I hold dear, yet it is not one rooted in the reality of my own upbringing. It is a path I have carefully crafted to offer my children a foundation different from the one I experienced. My childhood journey diverged sharply from this warmth and

Daddy, Let Go of My Hand

security, a landscape marked by absences, both physical and emotional, and too many complexities that I cannot summarize in a meaningful way for this book.

There are gaps in my own story that I often struggle to understand, fragments of memories and emotions that do not fit neatly into the narrative of a childhood I had hoped. My past, while shaping me in both good and bad ways, does not serve as the model I wish to follow. Instead, it has become the blueprint for what I want to avoid. When I think about what I want to give my children, I am guided less by experience than by a deep, instinctual desire to do things differently.

Sometimes, I wonder if the commitment I feel is enough. If my presence, my dedication to being there for every scraped knee, every tear, every laugh, will be enough to fill the gaps I fear might linger. I hope that my choice to be there every day, to listen, to sacrifice, and to show up with love, will lay the foundation for something secure and lasting. In a sense, my parenting is as much about what I hope to create as it is about what I strive to heal within myself. Each moment I spend with my children, each lesson I teach, each boundary I enforce, is part of a silent promise that I will do my best to be the parent I wish I had had.

I know that my children may never fully understand the weight of that promise, but they do not need to. What matters is that they feel loved, that they feel safe, and that they grow up knowing they have someone who believes in them, someone who would go to any lengths to see them thrive.

Chapter Two

Shadows of Self

Growing up, I did not have a clear picture of what I wanted, or even what was possible. So much of my identity was shaped by what I lacked, by what I observed in other families, in glimpses of what could be. I had no blueprint for the kind of parent I wanted to be, no lived experience of unconditional support or the quiet strength of a guiding hand. All I knew was that the life I wanted for my children did not yet exist. And if it did not exist, I would create it.

It sounds bold, even audacious, but it is the only way I know how to parent. If you want something that you have never had or if what you want does not exist in the world around you, you must create it yourself. There is no shortcut, no fallback. You become the source, the foundation, and the builder of the life you envision. I am reminded of the Nike slogan, *"impossible is nothing."* While it is a phrase so commonly repeated, it resonates deeply. For me, it is more than just motivation, it is the compass by which I measure my intentions.

I want my children to grow up with a sense of boundless possibility, the courage to carve their own path, and the belief that they can defy the limitations set before them. But creating that kind of environment is only half the battle. As children grow, they begin to discover the world beyond what their parents provide. They see how their own interests start to take form and become aware of the differences between who their parents envision them to be and who they feel themselves becoming.

It is a delicate time, both thrilling and unsettling for them and for me, as their dad. It is in this space, between who they are and who they might become, that self-doubt creeps in, where the ego begins to whisper, and where the seeds of identity start to take root.

Daddy, Let Go of My Hand

There is a bittersweet quality to watching them come into their own. They start to see the flaws in the image I worked so hard to build, to realize that I am not some untouchable, all-knowing figure. The mystery fades, and they begin to see me as I am, imperfect, often uncertain, and very human. The bond we have nurtured since birth is still there, but it is layered now with their emerging sense of self, a budding awareness that their lives are theirs to shape, just as mine is.

During this stage, they are caught between wanting to honor their family's legacy and wanting to break free from it. It is a challenging line to walk because, while they love and respect the world I have tried to create for them, they also feel the pull of their own visions, values, and dreams. Family pride, which once felt warm and reassuring, can also feel heavy, a burden to carry when they realize that becoming who they want to be may mean stepping outside of that pride or even challenging it.

The tension between family expectations and individual desires often breeds self-doubt. They start questioning whether they can live up to what I hope for them, or if they even want to. In the process, they come face-to-face with their own egos, the part of them that craves validation, approval, and acceptance. Reconciling these forces is never easy.

I see it in their eyes, in the way they wrestle with my expectations versus their own. I recognize it because I went through the same internal struggle myself, though for different reasons. My journey lacked a model for self-discovery, and now I am watching my children navigate a similar path, albeit from a more grounded place, with love and support that I hope will guide them forward.

One of the hardest lessons I have learned as a parent is that while I can offer guidance, I cannot make their choices for them. They are their own people, with their own dreams and ambitions. My role is not to shape them into an image of what I think is best, but rather to give them the freedom to explore, to stumble, and to rise again.

Daddy, Let Go of My Hand

As they explore who they are, they begin to imagine the person they want to become. They start envisioning their life, their values, their routines, and the things that matter most to them. They may not realize it yet, but in these small acts of self-discovery, they are laying the foundation for their future.

Routines, though seemingly mundane, are powerful tools for shaping character. Becoming the person, they want to be a grand leap but a gradual process, one that unfolds through daily choices.

I cannot help but marvel at how this process mirrors my own journey as a parent. Just as I am working to create a life I never had, they are building a vision of themselves, piece by piece, one day at a time. Parenting, too, is a daily practice of patience, understanding, and restraint.

There are days when I want to protect them from every hardship, to shield them from the self-doubt I know all too well. But I realize that doing so would deprive them of the strength that comes from facing challenges head-on.

This stage of their growth has been particularly difficult for me. We have shared so many years of closeness, of them looking to me as their compass and source of stability. Now, they are beginning to see the cracks, the parts of me that are flawed, human, and vulnerable.

They are learning that I am not a superhero, that I do not have all the answers, and that I am just as capable of missteps as they are. There is a certain sadness in that realization, but I understand that true love means letting go, even when it hurts.

In these moments, I hold onto the hope that my presence and dedication will be enough. That the foundation I have worked so hard to create will carry them through this transition. My hope is that they will emerge on the other side stronger, more self-assured, and ready to embrace the world with open hearts.

Daddy, Let Go of My Hand

Each day, I strive to create a space filled with values, resilience, kindness, integrity, and courage. These are not just words; they are the building blocks of a life on which they can rely. When life's winds blow strong, these values will function as an anchor, a place they can return to, repeatedly.

In those small, everyday moments, the shared meals, bedtime stories, laughter, and even tears. I am not just building memories; I am building invisible threads that tie them to their values, to each other, and to themselves.

As they move forward, discovering who they are and who they want to be, I am there, not as the all-knowing figure I once tried to be but as a steadfast presence, a quiet force in the background, cheering them on. And one day, they will look back and see that while I was not perfect, I was there doing my best to give them the life and love I never had.

In parenting, it is easy to get caught up in the future. But I have learned that the most powerful thing I can do is focus on the present. The future will unfold as it is meant to, but today, I can build the foundation for everything I hope they will carry with them.

With love as their foundation, I hope they will always have a sense of home, a place within themselves where they feel safe, capable, and deeply loved.

The journey of self-discovery is one of life's greatest balancing acts. For children, navigating the tension between honoring their DNA, the heritage, traits, and values passed down through generations, and forging their unique identity can want to walk a tightrope. On one side is the undeniable influence of family, a rich tapestry of history and tradition that shapes their foundation. On the other side is the equally compelling need to break free, explore, and create a life that is authentically theirs.

Honoring their DNA begins with understanding it. This means recognizing the strengths and

Daddy, Let Go of My Hand

limitations that come from their lineage. Children inherit more than just physical features; they carry the echoes of their family's values, beliefs, and even their struggles. Teaching them to value this inheritance is crucial. Parents can foster respect for their roots by sharing family stories, stories of resilience, sacrifice, and love. These narratives help children see that their DNA is not just a biological fact but a connection to something greater, a shared legacy that deserves recognition.

At the same time, children must learn that honoring their DNA does not mean being confined by it. They are not bound to repeat patterns or adopt values that no longer resonate. Encouraging them to forge their own identity means giving them the freedom to explore what truly matters to them. It involves allowing them to question family norms, challenge inherited beliefs, and carve out their own paths, even when those paths diverge from what their parents might envision.

The process of forging identity often begins with self-awareness. When children understand the qualities, they have inherited, whether it is their father's work ethic or their mother's creativity, they can decide how to integrate those traits into their lives. This integration is not an all-or-nothing choice. It is about selectively weaving together the parts of their heritage that align with their evolving sense of self, while respectfully leaving behind what does not.

Parents play a vital role in this delicate balance. They must model what it means to honor their own roots while embracing growth and change. By showing children that it is possible to love where you come from and still define where you are going, they create a blueprint for navigating this duality.

Honoring DNA while forging identity also requires children to embrace nuance. They are not one-

Daddy, Let Go of My Hand

dimensional beings shaped solely by biology or upbringing. They are dynamic individuals shaped by experience, environment, and choice. The plain fact of their DNA becomes a foundation, a starting point. Their identity is the structure they build upon it, layer by layer, shaped by their values, passions, and dreams.

Children honor their DNA by appreciating the legacy it represents while giving themselves permission to write their own story. It is a testament to the power of individuality, a reminder that even as we carry our ancestors with us, we are not bound by their footsteps. We are free to take our own.

Chapter Three

The Power of Time and Presence

When reflecting on life, it becomes clear that the people we meet often determine the paths we take. Some inspire us, others challenge us, and a few teach us lessons that last a lifetime. The key is learning to discern who deserves our energy and recognizing the profound impact of time spent with those who matter most.

My father, despite his good intentions, did not fully grasp the power of time. To him, time seemed to pass in unmeasured increments, yet the moments we shared during my childhood left an indelible mark. Though sparse, these scattered memories shaped me in ways I now understand and deeply value.

Daddy, Let Go of My Hand

Growing up with my paternal family, my interactions with my mother's side were limited and sporadic. This absence created a sense of longing and curiosity about relationships I never fully experienced. That longing taught me to cherish the time I do have with loved ones. It became a guiding principle in my own parenting: to be present and intentional with my children, ensuring they never feel the same void I once did.

One of the most profound pieces of advice I have received came from my stepmother. She emphasized the importance of creating a safe space for my children, one where they feel free to share anything without fear of judgment or rejection. Her wisdom has become a cornerstone of my parenting philosophy, reminding my children that my love for them surpasses any temporary frustrations.

My wife embodies a quiet strength through her remarkable patience and non-reactivity. Her calm demeanor has shown me the value of measured responses, reminding me that reacting to every situation dilutes the impact of my attention. Her example encourages me to approach life with intentionality and grace, lessons I hope to pass down to our children.

Time is the ultimate currency, finite and irreplaceable. How we spend it defines our relationships and shapes our legacy. Through the intentional use of time with my family, I have come to understand that presence is not just physical; it is emotional and spiritual. These shared moments become the foundation of a bond that endures beyond a lifetime.

Contrary to popular belief, we are not prisoners of our past. Creativity and imagination allow us to reimagine our futures. By nurturing desire and tapping into our imagination, we can break free from old cycles and build lives filled with purpose and joy. The ability to dream is not limited to childhood; it is a skill that strengthens with practice and a powerful tool for shaping our reality.

The moments we invest in love, patience, and openness create a foundation for the next generation. My hope is that the lessons I have

Daddy, Let Go of My Hand

learned from my father, stepmother, and wife, will anchor my children, equipping them with the resilience and confidence to navigate life's challenges. This legacy of presence and purpose is my greatest gift to them.

As I reflect on this journey, I am deeply grateful for the relationships that have shaped me and the opportunity to be present for my loved ones. Each moment is a chance to strengthen these bonds, to create memories that matter, and to build a life rooted in love, patience, and imagination.

Time is a gift, and how we use it defines the story we leave behind. For my family, for myself, and for those yet to come, I strive to make every moment count.

Chapter Four

Balancing Dreams and Expectations

As children grow and begin to find their voices, it is natural for a power struggle to arise between them and their parents. What starts as an unshakable bond of dependence and guidance can evolve into a delicate dance of autonomy and control. Children, in their quest for identity, often push against the boundaries set by their parents, testing limits and asserting independence. For parents, this phase can be unsettling, a stark departure from the early years when their guidance felt unquestioned.

This struggle is not only inevitable but also vital. It is a sign that a child is maturing, seeking to understand their place in the world. For parents, the

Daddy, Let Go of My Hand

challenge lies in striking the right balance: respecting their child's independence while continuing to guide them toward a foundation of life skills, habits, and values that will serve them well.

Life skills and values are not innate; they are cultivated over time. Parents play a crucial role in this process, teaching resilience, patience, hard work, and responsibility. These lessons are imparted not just through words but through actions, modeling behaviors they hope their children will adopt. However, as children begin to assert their own ideas and aspirations, the question arises: How do parents ensure they are nurturing, not imposing?

This tension becomes particularly pronounced when a parent's unfulfilled dreams enter the equation. It is a human tendency to project our hopes and regrets onto those closest to us, especially our children. We might see their potential as an opportunity to correct our own missed chances, blurring the line between supporting their growth and pursuing our ambitions through them.

Consider the story of a father who once aspired to be a professional baseball player. His dream was set aside when life's responsibilities called for a different path. Years later, watching his child show a natural talent for sport stirs something deep within him, a mix of pride, hope, and longing. Encouraging his child to develop this talent feels both natural and urgent. But as he invests time, energy, and resources into their training, a question arises: Whose dream is he truly nurturing?

This scenario highlights a common parental dilemma. While pushing a child to realize their potential can be beneficial, it is essential to discern whether that push aligns with the child's own desires. Motivation must come from within, and when it does not, external pressure risks breeding resentment instead of growth.

Parents often unconsciously project their unresolved feelings onto their children. Frustration with a child's perceived lack of drive might stem from the parent's own regrets or unfulfilled ambitions. Recognizing this dynamic requires self-

Daddy, Let Go of My Hand

awareness and humility. It is a chance to ask difficult but necessary questions:

Am I guiding them for their benefit or for mine? Am I helping them pursue their dreams or trying to rewrite my story through them?

This self-reflection can be uncomfortable but transformative. By acknowledging their motivations, parents can create space for their children to explore their individuality. It is a reminder that their role is not to mold their child into a replica of themselves but to support them in becoming their own person.

Empathy is a powerful tool in navigating these challenges. It requires parents to set aside their assumptions and truly listen to their child's perspective. This does not mean relinquishing all guidance; rather, it means being attuned to their child's feelings, motivations, and goals. Empathy builds trust and opens the door to meaningful conversations, fostering a relationship based on mutual respect rather than control.

When parents practice empathy, they create a space where their child feels seen and valued. This approach not only strengthens the parent-child bond but also equips the child with the confidence to explore their identity and make choices that align with their values.

As children assert their independence, boundaries become essential. For the child, setting boundaries is a way to define their identity and explore their autonomy. For the parents, it is a humbling reminder that their role is shifting. Boundaries can be challenging, often leading to friction, but they are also an opportunity for growth. They teach children to stand firm in their beliefs while allowing parents to evolve into a role of mutual respect.

Pride and confidence are central themes in this dynamic. Parents take pride in their children's growth and accomplishments, but pride can also blind them to their child's individuality. Similarly, children navigate their own pride balancing the need for independence with the deep desire for parental approval.

Daddy, Let Go of My Hand

This push-and-pull creates moments of vulnerability for both parties. Parents must learn to let go of the need to control, trusting their children to find their own way. Children, in turn, must learn to navigate their independence without losing sight of the values instilled in them.

The relationship between parent and child is ever evolving. As children grow, they challenge their parents to reflect, adapt, and grow alongside them. This journey is not without its struggles, but it is through these challenges that both sides come to appreciate each other as individuals.

The goal is not to dictate a child's path but to walk alongside them, offering guidance and support as they navigate life's complexities. By balancing dreams with expectations, pride with empathy, and guidance with freedom, parents can create a relationship that honors both their hopes and their child's individuality. Together, they can build a foundation of mutual respect and shared confidence, a partnership that allows both to thrive.

Chapter Five

Embracing Independence

There is a moment in every parent's journey that feels both heart-wrenching and deeply fulfilling, a bittersweet rite of passage when you realize it is time to step back. The child, once so reliant on your guidance, is ready to embrace their independence. The familiarity of your role as a protector begins to dissolve, replaced by something more tenuous yet profound: trust. This transition, while natural and necessary, can want to navigate uncharted territory for both the parent and the child.

For fathers, this journey often begins with subtle realizations: fewer questions, less reliance on advice, and a growing confidence in their child's steps. Each moment of self-sufficiency is a triumph, but it also brings a quiet ache, a reminder that your

Daddy, Let Go of My Hand

presence in their life will begin to change in ways you cannot fully control. As fathers, we long to stay close, to protect, to remain a steady anchor. But part of true love is knowing when to give space, trusting that they can manage what lies ahead.

This is not a straightforward process. Letting go requires setting aside the familiar role of constant guide and protector, becoming instead a source of quiet support from the sidelines. Watching them take risks, stumble, and soar, all without your intervention, is both terrifying and exhilarating. It is an opportunity to witness the person they are becoming, shaped not only by your influence but by their own dreams, decisions, and experiences.

For the child, this transition is equally transformative. As they step out into the world, they carry the lessons and values of their upbringing but face the unknown on their own terms. The thrill of independence is tempered by the awareness that they are leaving behind the safety of a constant, loving presence. Yet in this process, they build something new: a sense of self shaped by their choices and the courage to chart their path.

The father's role shifts from teacher to observer, a quiet yet steady presence. Letting go means finding peace in the unknown, trusting that the roots you have nurtured are strong enough to support them as they grow. It means accepting that you cannot shield them from every misstep or guide every decision. Instead, you believe in the resilience and wisdom they have developed over the years.

This journey teaches both father and child invaluable lessons. The father learns to relinquish control, finding joy in witnessing his child's courage. The child learns the thrill and weight of independence, navigating a world that will evaluate their strength and character. The relationship evolves, grounded not in dependency but in mutual respect and admiration.

The pain of letting go is softened by the pride of seeing them forge a life that is truly their own. Watching them succeed, falter, and grow reveals the enduring impact of the values and love you have

Daddy, Let Go of My Hand

instilled. This foundation becomes a compass, guiding them as they explore their potential and purpose.

In this transition, father and child redefine their bond. For the father, it is about stepping back with grace, offering encouragement without overshadowing their autonomy. For the child, it is a moment of ownership, assessing the wings they have been building and learning to fly.

This process is not without its challenges. There will be moments of doubt, hesitation, and the occasional return for reassurance. There will also be moments when the father longs to intervene. But the strength of this transition lies in the foundation they have built together a bond that remains strong even as the child ventures into the unknown.

With time, the child begins to see their father in a new light. As life teaches its own lessons through experience and struggle, the early teachings and values become clearer. What once felt like rules or expectations are now understood as tools for thriving independently. The father's presence, though quieter, remains a steady force, a reminder of the love and sacrifices that helped shape their journey.

As the child matures, the relationship transforms. The father becomes less an instructor and more a confidant, a source of wisdom and support. The child's successes and struggles are no longer met with directives but with quiet pride and understanding. The early years, softened by time, become cherished memories, a foundation for the deeper bond that now exists.

Letting go is not an end; it is a beginning. It is the start of a new chapter in the relationship, one built on trust and mutual respect. It is an acknowledgment that love does not diminish with distance; it grows stronger as both father and child learn to appreciate each other's individuality.

As the father watches his child step fully into independence, he finds solace in knowing that his influence remains. The values, lessons, and love are carried forward, shaping not just who they are but

Daddy, Let Go of My Hand

the life they are building. In this way, the father's presence endures, not as a guiding hand but as a steadying force that will always be part of their journey.

This is the beauty of embracing independence: a celebration of growth, courage, and the unbreakable bond between a father and child. While the process may be bittersweet, it is also a profound reminder of love's ability to evolve, deepen, and endure through every stage of life.

Chapter Six

Hopes, Fears, and the Future Unseen

As a parent, you constantly tread a fine line between cherishing the milestones of the past, grappling with the uncertainties of the present, and anticipating the mysteries of the future. Parenting is an act of perpetual balance both exhilarating and daunting. The future stretches ahead like an endless horizon, brimming with both promise and potential pitfalls. In this delicate dance of preparation and surrender, you guide your child through today's challenges while equipping them for a world you cannot fully imagine.

Every parent wrestles with the same questions, over and over: *What* obstacles will my child face that I cannot foresee? What values can I instill to prepare

Daddy, Let Go of My Hand

them for a future I cannot predict? And how can I teach them to meet life's inevitable changes with resilience and courage?

This chapter is about navigating those questions, embracing uncertainty, and finding strength in the hopes and fears that define your parenting journey.

Looking back, the concerns that once felt so enormous now seem laughably small. The first day of school, learning to make friends, the tears shed over scraped knees or nighttime fears these were once your world. You stood as their protector, their unwavering guide through every stumble. With a reassuring hug or a whispered *"It'll be okay,"* you gave them the courage to face the small struggles of childhood.

Yet as they grow, these worries evolve into challenges far beyond your immediate control. Academic pressures, social dynamics, the influence of peers, and the complexities of growing independence now demand more than simple reassurances. You begin to realize that your role is no longer just to shield them but to prepare them to equip them with tools they can carry into an unpredictable future.

The innocence of yesterday's worries gives way to the weight of what lies ahead. It is a bittersweet transition, but it is also a reminder of the strength they have already gained from the foundation you have laid.

The future is unknowable, and that truth is both terrifying and exhilarating. Your child will enter a world shaped by technologies, challenges, and global shifts that you cannot fully grasp. The pace of change is dizzying faster than at any point in human history and with it comes uncertainty.

Yet within this uncertainty lies opportunity. It is through adaptation and resilience that extraordinary individuals are born. Those who learn to thrive amidst change are the ones who leave a lasting impact on the world. As a parent, your role is to guide your child to see not just the obstacles but also the boundless possibilities that lie ahead.

Daddy, Let Go of My Hand

The unknown is not a void to be feared but a canvas waiting for them to paint their own masterpiece.

Though you cannot control what lies ahead, you can arm your child with a compass. Certain timeless values, adaptability, curiosity, empathy, perseverance, and integrity will function as their guiding lights, no matter how the world shifts around them.

Change is the only constant. Teach them to see it as an opportunity, not a threat. An adaptable mind can navigate uncharted waters and find new paths where none seem to exist.

Encourage them to ask questions, to wonder, and to seek understanding. A curious mind is a growing mind, one that embraces challenges as puzzles waiting to be solved.

In a world increasingly connected yet deeply divided, empathy is their bridge to understanding and connection. Teach them to see through the eyes of others and to value perspectives different from their own.

The ability to keep going in the face of failure is the most important trait of all. Life will evaluate them, but perseverance will help them rise, learn, and continue their journey.

The foundation of trust and respect, and integrity will anchor them in a world filled with shifting values. Teach them to stand firm in their beliefs and to act with honor, even when it is difficult.

These values will be their tools not to solve every problem for them but to empower them to face whatever challenges arise.

It is easy to focus on the obstacles your child will face. But as much as the future holds challenges, it also offers unprecedented opportunities. This generation has access to knowledge, technologies, and global connections that were once unimaginable. They can champion causes, create innovations, and build communities that embrace diversity and progress.

Your role is to inspire them to see these possibilities. Show them the beauty of curiosity, the power of resilience, and the fulfillment that comes from pursuing a life of integrity. Teach them to view the unknown not as something to fear but as an invitation to grow and dream.

The future is an open road. Help them take the first step with confidence and purpose.

As your child grows, the time will come when you must step back and let them take the reins of their own life. This is the most challenging lesson of all: your love and guidance were always meant to prepare them for a life lived independently.

It is natural to want to shield them, to keep guiding them through every challenge. But to truly empower them, you must let go. Trust that you have given them the tools they need and that they will find their way, even if it is different from the path, you might have chosen for them.

Letting go does not mean stepping away. You will always be there, a steady presence, ready to cheer them on or catch them if they fall. But this is their journey, not yours.

In the end, your hopes for them are both simple and profound. You hope they are happy. You hope they find meaning in their lives, that they build relationships founded on love and respect, and that they are effective in the world.

You hope they have the courage to chase their dreams, the resilience to overcome setbacks, and the wisdom to know that failure is not the end but a steppingstone to growth.

The future is unseen, but it is also unwritten. And with every value you have instilled, every lesson you have taught, and every ounce of love you have given, you have helped prepare them to author their own extraordinary story.

In that, you can find peace. For in your child, the hopes of tomorrow shine brightly, ready to illuminate the world.

Chapter Seven

Fostering Independence: The Greatest Gift a Parent Can Give

The most profound lesson any parent can instruct their child is the art of independence. This lesson, when imparted thoughtfully and consistently, serves as a foundation upon which the child can build a meaningful, self-reliant life. Teaching independence is akin to teaching a person how to fish: if you only provide for your child, giving them everything they need but never showing them how to meet those needs themselves, they may come to rely on you indefinitely. However, if you teach them how to "fish," they gain the skills and confidence needed to meet their needs, whether they are emotional, intellectual, or practical.

In our materialistic world, it is easy to equate love with the things we give. A parent might feel tempted to buy their child every toy, gadget, or material desire, thinking these gifts will create happiness and security. But material things, no matter how abundant, cannot replace the truly valuable and lasting things in life. As much as buying a child everything they want may feel like an expression of love, it does not teach them about the enduring values that matter most. Love and support must be reflected through nurturing independence, providing emotional and intellectual nourishment, and modeling the values children will carry for the rest of their lives.

True love is not about sheltering children from all discomfort or handing them every convenience; it is about empowering them to navigate the world with resilience, empathy, and a sense of purpose. Teaching independence starts with modeling self-sufficiency in a loving environment, where the child feels safe enough to explore the world yet confident enough to manage setbacks.

Daddy, Let Go of My Hand

A child learns from what they see and feel. When they see a parent taking on challenges, solving problems, and exhibiting patience in the face of adversity, they internalize these behaviors as part of their understanding of adulthood. Independence does not mean cold detachment; it is about balancing warmth and support with opportunities to gain experience. When children understand they are unconditionally loved, they are more likely to take on challenges and risk failure, knowing they have a haven to return to.

Unconditional love is not a material gift, it does not come with a price tag. But it instills in children a sense of self-worth that cannot be taken away. It is a gift that teaches them they are worthy of respect, care, and happiness, which is the cornerstone of a healthy and independent adulthood.

Raising an independent child involves equipping them with the tools to make sense of the world. This does not necessarily mean filling their heads with data; it is about cultivating curiosity and a love for learning. Teaching children how to learn rather than what to learn has a lasting impact. When a child is curious, they learn to seek out knowledge on their own. They become lifelong learners, which is a hallmark of independence.

This means encouraging questions rather than providing immediate answers and fostering an environment where it is okay not to know but to want to find out. For example, if a child asks why the sky is blue, a parent can respond, "That is a great question! Let us explore it together," rather than offering a ready-made answer. In doing so, you are not just teaching them a fact; you are teaching them the joy of discovery and the satisfaction of curiosity.

As they grow, they may face more complex situations, but if they have learned the skill of inquiry, they will know where and how to find the answers they need. This confidence in their ability to seek out knowledge and solutions is the essence of intellectual independence.

In addition to intellectual independence, children also need a strong moral and ethical foundation. Values are the compass by which they will navigate life's many challenges. Without values, independence can easily become self-centered or misguided; with values, it becomes purposeful and conscientious.

Values such as empathy, kindness, honesty, and resilience cannot be purchased or drilled into a child through force or rewards. Instead, they are cultivated through example. When children see their parents acting with integrity, being honest even when it is difficult, or showing kindness in challenging situations, they learn these behaviors firsthand.

Teaching empathy, for instance, means showing children how to care for others and consider their feelings. If a child grows up seeing their parents volunteer, stand up for fairness, or show compassion to those in need, they learn that these qualities are integral to a meaningful life. Resilience, another crucial value, equips children to manage setbacks and continue moving forward. Parents model resilience by facing hardships with determination and accepting failure as part of growth.

Independence, knowledge, and values can only be taught if parents dedicate time to their children. Quality time is not just about being physically present; it is about being mentally and emotionally available, fully engaged with the child's thoughts, experiences, and growth. These moments allow parents to observe and understand their child's unique personality, strengths, and areas where they need guidance.

In a world full of distractions, time can feel like a luxury, but it is one of the few luxuries that cannot be bought or replaced. When parents spend quality time with their children, they may not remember every toy or gadget they were given, but they will remember the feeling of being loved, heard, and appreciated. This emotional security becomes a permanent part of who they are.

When parents strive to teach independence, they are not only preparing their children for adulthood but also giving them a gift that lasts a lifetime.

Daddy, Let Go of My Hand

Independence means having the confidence to pursue goals, the skills to learn continuously, and the moral compass to make meaningful choices. These qualities become an enduring part of their identity.

Parents who teach independence teach their children that they are capable and deserving of a fulfilling life. While there will be times when they stumble or face difficulties, the lessons of independence give them the tools to rise again.

Teaching independence becomes not only a gift to the child but also a contribution to the world, a future filled with capable, compassionate, and resilient individuals who enrich the lives of those around them.

Chapter Eight

Building a Foundation of Safety, Security, and Real-World Education

As a parent, your goal is often simple yet profound: to help our children thrive. At the heart of this goal lies the need to create a world in which they feel safe and secure. It is easy to become consumed by aspirations for their success, selecting the right schools, enrolling them in the best activities, and cheering for their accomplishments. Yet beneath all these ambitions lies a foundation that is far more essential. Safety and security form the bedrock upon which all future growth depends. Without this foundation, everything else becomes shaky, and a child's ability to reach their potential is compromised.

Daddy, Let Go of My Hand

A child who feels safe and secure can explore the world with confidence, knowing they have a home base of love, acceptance, and support. This sense of security is not only rooted in physical shelter but also in emotional safety. It comes from consistent reassurance, steady routines, and the enduring presence of parents who are there, day in and day out. This chapter explores how to build that foundation and expand it beyond traditional education to equip children for life's complexities.

In many societies, the belief that education is the key to success is deeply ingrained. While this is true to an extent, education can open doors and create opportunities, the traditional schooling system falls short in preparing children for the broader challenges of life. Schools focus heavily on academics, which, while valuable, are only one piece of the puzzle.

The traditional classroom environment was designed with a primary purpose: to prepare students for the workforce. It emphasizes structure, routine, and standardized outcomes. Students are taught to follow instructions, meet deadlines, and conform to expectations. While these skills are important, they do not necessarily foster independent thinking, resilience, or creativity.

Critical thinking, for example, is often undervalued in the traditional educational system. Students are rewarded for reproducing expected answers rather than challenging assumptions or exploring alternative perspectives. This creates competent workers but does not always nurture the innovative analytical people or compassionate leaders our world desperately needs.

True education extends far beyond the boundaries of a classroom. It is in the real world that children learn the lessons that will carry them through life. Values like honesty, integrity, resilience, and kindness are not taught in textbooks, they are absorbed through experience, observation, and guidance.

A child learns kindness by witnessing it in their family interactions. They develop resilience through facing setbacks and learning to recover from failure.

Daddy, Let Go of My Hand

Integrity becomes a cornerstone when they observe the adults around them making difficult, ethical choices. These lessons cannot be quantified by test scores, but they are essential in shaping a well-rounded individual prepared to navigate life's complexities.

Furthermore, life's unpredictable nature presents challenges that cannot be captured in a classroom setting. A child's ability to adapt, think critically, and respond with courage and resilience is what will define their success and happiness. By emphasizing real-world education and practical skills, we prepare our children for the uncertainties of adulthood.

The environment children grow up in shapes their views and influences their choices, but a sturdy foundation built on love, security, and guiding values gives them something to return to, no matter where life takes them. This foundation is not built in a single moment. It is the product of countless small interactions that instill a sense of worth, belonging, and purpose.

Children who feel grounded in a stable home environment are better equipped to weather life's storms. They can question the world around them, embrace challenges with curiosity, and take risks knowing they have a secure base to fall back on. This security is not a luxury; it is a necessity for healthy emotional and intellectual development.

The goal of parenting is not to raise children who simply meet expectations but to nurture individuals who are independent thinkers and compassionate contributors to society. This requires giving children the space to explore, ask questions, and make mistakes. Strength of character comes from understanding one's own values, standing by those values, and learning from life's challenges.

Developing independence is not a sudden act but a gradual process. Children learn responsibility by being trusted with age-appropriate tasks. They gain confidence when their opinions are valued, and they grow through the experience of making decisions both good and bad. These lessons instill both self-

Daddy, Let Go of My Hand

assurance and humility, qualities that are essential for a successful and fulfilling life.

The world is evolving at an unprecedented pace, and the future our children will face is vastly different from the one we know. With rapid advancements in technology, globalization, and societal shifts, the skills they will need are continually changing. As parents, we cannot predict every challenge they will encounter, but we can equip them with the tools to adapt and thrive.

Preparing children for the future is not about providing all the answers but teaching them how to ask the right questions. It is about encouraging curiosity, critical thinking, and a love of lifelong learning. When children have a foundation of security and are equipped to think independently and act with integrity, they can navigate an uncertain future with confidence.

The greatest gift we can give our children is the foundation that allows them to build a life beyond the boundaries we set. A foundation rooted in safety, love, and values empowers them to face the world with courage, knowing they have an unshakable base to draw upon.

Traditional education is just one aspect of their preparation. Real education, the one that happens through life experiences and family guidance, shapes them into resilient, thoughtful, and compassionate individuals. Letting go does not mean stepping away; it means standing by, ready to support, guide, and love them as they forge their path.

By creating a foundation of safety, security, and real-world education, we prepare our children not only to succeed but to thrive in a world full of possibilities. In doing so, we empower them to build a future they can proudly call their own.

Chapter Nine

Reflection and Reconciliation

Every father who has been present and actively involved in raising their children can recall moments of bittersweet revelation, those instances when the passage of time and the growth of a child become undeniably clear. It is a scene replayed in countless ways across generations, yet it feels deeply personal and profound each time. It happens when your child takes their first independent ride on a bike, confidently calling out, "Look, Dad, I'm doing it with no hands!" Or it is the quiet determination in their eyes when, as they learn to walk, they push away from your steadying grip, silently declaring, "Dad, let go of my hands!"

These milestones are not just moments of achievement for the child, they are transformative for the father as well. They signify a pivotal shift, a step toward independence that evokes equal parts, pride, and nostalgia. Watching your child take those first steps or steer through their first wobbly ride fills you with joy and satisfaction. Yet, there is also an undeniable pang, a small ache that accompanies the realization that they are beginning to need you less in the ways they once did.

These moments, both exhilarating and humbling, offer fathers an opportunity for deep reflection. They prompt us to look back on the journey,

the scraped knees, the tears of frustration, the encouraging words, and the triumphant cheers. Each stumble and recovery, each push and steadying hand, has been part of a larger narrative: the gradual unfolding of a child's independence. And in these memories, fathers find the profound truth that their role has always been about preparing their children to stand on their own.

Daddy, Let Go of My Hand

The acts of teaching a child to walk, to ride, or to face life's challenges are not just about those specific skills. They are lessons in resilience, courage, and self-reliance. Each "let go" moment is a leap of faith, not just for the child but for the father as well. In releasing their hand or letting them pedal on their own, you are trusting in the foundation you have helped build, confident that it will carry them forward.

These experiences reveal the unspoken contract between parent and child: trust. For the child, trust is in your presence, your guidance, and your readiness to catch them if they fall. For the father, trust is in their strength, their ability to rise, and their determination to try again. This mutual trust forms the cornerstone of the relationship, creating a bond that is both enduring and transformative.

Fatherhood often involves reconciling two opposing desires: the instinct to protect and the need to let go. It is a balancing act, one that demands constant adaptation and self-awareness. In moments of reflection, fathers come to terms with this tension, realizing that true love is not about holding on too tightly but about preparing their children to thrive independently.

This reconciliation is not always easy. It requires fathers to confront their own fears,

the fear of no longer being needed, the fear of seeing their child stumble, and the fear of letting them face the world's uncertainties. But through this process, fathers discover a deeper truth: that their role is not to shield their children from every hardship but to equip them with the tools to overcome those challenges.

In letting go, fathers allow their children to step into their own strength and embrace their own journey. This act of stepping back is not a withdrawal of love or support but an affirmation of belief in their child's potential. It is a humbling realization, one that redefines what it means to be a father.

As fathers, we learn and grow alongside our children. Just as they are learning to navigate the world, we are learning to navigate the complexities

Daddy, Let Go of My Hand

of parenthood. Each stage of their development presents new challenges and new opportunities for growth. Fatherhood, it turns out, is not a fixed role but a dynamic journey marked by cycles of holding on and letting go.

These cycles bring moments of profound clarity. Fathers realize that their presence, even in the smallest acts, steadying a bike, wiping away tears, or cheering from the sidelines, has left an indelible mark. The qualities they have nurtured in their children, resilience, courage, and independence, will serve them well as they face the challenges of adulthood. And in recognizing this, fathers find a quiet sense of pride and purpose.

Even as the nature of fatherhood evolves, the bond between father and child remains unbreakable. It shifts and transforms, but it is never diminished. Fathers become a steady presence in the background, ready to offer guidance when needed but equally willing to watch from a distance as their children soar.

This enduring connection is a testament to the love and trust that have been cultivated over the years. It is a bond built on moments of shared joy, mutual respect, and unwavering belief in one another. And as fathers reflect on these moments, they find solace in knowing that their love and influence will always be part of their child's journey.

Fatherhood is about giving and receiving gifts that transcend the physical. The greatest gift a father can offer his child is the confidence to declare, "Look, Dad, I'm doing it on my own." And the greatest gift a child can give their father is the trust that made letting go possible.

Through this journey of reflection and reconciliation, fathers find peace in knowing that they have done their part. They have given their children the strength to rise, the courage to explore, and the belief in their own potential. Though they may no longer be holding them steady, their presence, love, and guidance remain, offering silent support as their children continue forward, one step, one pedal, one leap at a time.

Daddy, Let Go of My Hand

Parenting is never about perfect precision. It is not an academic exercise where every action has a guaranteed outcome, nor does it require exactitude in balancing protection and letting go. Instead, it is a deeply personal journey, full of trial and error, adjustments, and moments of self-discovery. As dassies, we quickly learn that this balance is not static, it shifts with time, circumstances, and the evolving needs of our children.

The art of being a daddy lies in embracing this imperfection. There will be times when we lean too far into protection, holding on tightly out of fear of what the world might bring. At other times, we may let go too quickly, driven by the desire to see our children thrive on their own. Neither approach is inherently wrong; each reflects love and care. The key is to be attuned to when adjustments are needed and to approach the process with humility and grace.

Children, in their beautiful imperfection, remind us that parenting is not about exactitude, it is about intention. When we act with love, our mistakes are softened by the trust we have built. They forgive our overprotectiveness when they see it stems from concern, and they appreciate the moments we step back, even when we're unsure if they're ready.

Balancing protection and letting go does not require academic precision; it requires presence. It is in the quiet moments, watching them struggle with a difficult task but resisting the urge to step in, or offering advice while knowing they may not take it, that we learn to navigate this balance. These moments are not about finding the perfect answer but about showing up, being present, and trusting in the foundation we have built.

Letting go does not mean abandoning our role; it means evolving within it. We transition from

Daddy, Let Go of My Hand

holding their hand to standing beside them, from leading the way to cheering them on from the sidelines. The balance is never fixed, and that is okay. What matters is the love that guides our decisions and the willingness to adapt as our children grow into the independent individuals they are meant to be.

The balance between protection and letting go is not about academic exactitude, it is about embracing the messy, beautiful, and deeply human experience of parenthood. It is about trusting our instincts, forgiving our missteps, and celebrating the milestones that mark our children's journey into adulthood. And in those moments when we get it right, however fleeting, we glimpse the profound impact of our love and presence in their lives.

Chapter Ten

Building a Foundation for a Better Future

In a world increasingly focused on personal success and individual fulfillment, the notion of setting children up for a better future often becomes intertwined with the concept of privilege. However, the two are not synonymous. Privilege can be circumstantial and fleeting, whereas a solid foundation for a child's life is enduring and deeply rooted. It requires more than material wealth or societal advantages; it demands intentional and consistent investment in their emotional, moral, and relational well-being.

Creating this foundation begins with principles that transcend cultural and economic differences. At its core, it requires parents and caregivers to provide a

Daddy, Let Go of My Hand

nurturing environment where love, values, and support pave the way for a child's growth. This chapter explores the key components necessary for equipping children with the tools they need to thrive, not just in the present but throughout their lives.

A child's first and most profound experience of love and security comes from their parents. When a mother and father are not only present but also demonstrate love and mutual respect, they create a stable environment where children feel safe. This foundation sets the tone for how children will perceive relationships, conflict resolution, and emotional stability in their own lives.

Parental presence goes beyond physical availability. It encompasses emotional engagement, active listening, and participation in their child's daily life. When parents model a loving and respectful partnership, children internalize these behaviors, learning the importance of empathy, communication, and collaboration.

Children flourish when they grow up with clear moral values and a sense of purpose. Teaching right from wrong is not merely about enforcing rules; it is about instilling a compass that guides them through life's complexities. Moral values, honesty, kindness, integrity, and responsibility, serve as anchors during times of uncertainty and temptation.

Equally important is encouraging children to set and pursue goals. Goal orientation teaches perseverance, focus, and the value of hard work. When paired with a system of earned rewards, children learn to appreciate the connection between effort and achievement. The experience of earning rather than receiving instills pride, confidence, and a robust work ethic that will benefit them throughout their lives.

At the heart of every child's development lies the need for unconditional love. This love is not contingent on accomplishments, behavior, or conformity but is given freely and without reservation. When children know they are loved unconditionally, they develop a sense of security

Daddy, Let Go of My Hand

that enables them to explore the world with confidence and resilience.

Support and encouragement are equally critical. They help children navigate challenges, celebrate victories, and learn from failures. Parents and caregivers who provide consistent encouragement foster an environment where children feel empowered to take risks, pursue their passions, and embrace their individuality.

While parents play a central role, children thrive when surrounded by a broader community of love and support. This "army" can include extended family members, teachers, mentors, neighbors, and friends who invest in the child's life. A diverse network of caring individuals provides children with multiple perspectives, opportunities for growth, and a deeper sense of belonging.

This community also acts as a safety net, offering guidance and encouragement during difficult times. The collective love and investment of many people help children feel valued and supported, reinforcing their sense of self-worth and potential.

Parenting is an act of selfless love. The sacrifices made for children, the time, effort, resources, and emotional energy, are not transactions. They are investments made without expectation of repayment. When parents release their children from the burden of "owing" them, they create a space where children can pursue their dreams without guilt or obligation.

This principle fosters gratitude rather than resentment. Children who grow up knowing their parents' love and support are unconditional are more likely to give freely to others, perpetuating a cycle of generosity and kindness.

Setting children up for a better future is about creating a foundation that equips them to navigate life with confidence, resilience, and a sense of purpose. It requires intentional effort to build an environment grounded in love, values, and community support. It also demands a selfless approach, where the goal is the child's flourishing rather than the parent's gain.

When parents and caregivers embrace these principles, they give their children a gift far more valuable than privilege, a life rooted in strength, love, and the ability to thrive, no matter the challenges they may face.

The early years of a child's life are the bedrock upon which their future is built. To cultivate strong roots and bonds with young children, it is essential to understand the difference between simply fulfilling a role and embracing the privilege of parenting. The distinction between being a "father" and being a "daddy," as explored earlier, is a profound one. It illustrates the importance of not just being present but being purposeful in that presence. This chapter delves into actionable strategies to foster deep connections with children, ensuring they grow up rooted in love, trust, and security.

The foundation of any relationship is built on presence, but not just physical presence, intentional presence. Children thrive when they know that their caregiver is genuinely interested in their world. Being intentional means carving out dedicated time to engage with your child. It is about putting aside distractions, whether it is work, technology, or other responsibilities, and focusing entirely on them.

Establish a daily routine that includes undivided attention for your child, even if it is just 15 minutes of playtime, storytelling, or a simple conversation about their day. Consistency builds trust and signals that they are a priority.

Children often understand love more through actions than words. While it is important to say, "I love you," it is equally crucial to show it. This can take the form of small gestures, like preparing their favorite snack, being patient during tantrums, or creating traditions that make them feel special.

Create rituals that celebrate your relationship, such as a special handshake, weekly family game nights,

Daddy, Let Go of My Hand

or bedtime routines that include shared prayers or stories.

To build strong roots, children need to feel emotionally secure. This means being a haven where they can express their feelings without fear of judgment or dismissal. When children know, they can come to you with anything, it strengthens their trust and deepens the bond.

Practice active listening. When your child shares something, stop what you are doing, get on their eye level, and listen attentively. Acknowledge their emotions with validating phrases like, "I see you are upset, and that is okay. Let us talk about it."

Discipline, when rooted in love, becomes a tool for teaching rather than punishment. Setting boundaries and enforcing them teaches children about responsibility and self-control, but it must be balanced with nurturing, which ensures they feel valued and supported.

Use positive discipline techniques. For example, instead of saying, "Don't do that," try, "Let's do this instead." Reinforce good behavior with praise and explain the reasoning behind rules to help them understand.

Children learn more from what you do than what you say. They observe how you manage stress, interact with others, and approach life's challenges. To cultivate strong roots, model the behavior and values you wish to instill in them.

Practice self-regulation. If you want your child to manage frustration calmly, demonstrate this by managing your own emotions constructively. Apologize when you make mistakes, showing them that accountability is a strength.

Shared experiences form the glue of a strong parent-child bond. These memories do not have to be extravagant; even simple moments, like baking cookies, going on a nature walk, or working on a project together, can become cherished memories.

Dedicate time for family activities. Whether it is an annual camping trip or a weekend picnic, these moments provide a sense of continuity and joy.

Daddy, Let Go of My Hand

As much as children need nurturing, they also need guidance. It is a delicate balance of giving them the freedom to explore and grow while providing the structure they need to feel safe.

Encourage independence by offering choices. For example, "Would you like to wear the blue shirt or the red one today?" This helps them feel empowered while still maintaining boundaries.

Trust is the cornerstone of any strong relationship. For children, trust comes from knowing they can rely on you. This means following through on promises, being consistent in your rules, and showing up when they need you.

If you promise to do something, make it a priority to follow through. Whether it is attending a school event or playing a game, keeping your word reinforces trust.

Every child is unique, with their own personality, interests, and pace of development. Celebrating their individuality helps them feel valued and respected.

Take time to discover your child's interests and strengths. If they love drawing, provide art supplies, and praise their creativity. Let them know you see and appreciate them for who they are.

Parenting is as much about self-growth as it is about raising a child. Reflecting on your own upbringing and experiences can help you identify patterns to replicate or break. As shared earlier, the desire to create a different path for your children can be a powerful motivator.

Write a parenting journal. Reflect on what is working, what challenges your face, and how you can improve. This self-awareness will guide you in becoming the parent you aspire to be.

Parenting is a journey filled with difficulties. Mistakes are inevitable, both for you and your child. Demonstrating forgiveness and patience teaches them that love is unconditional and that mistakes are opportunities for growth.

When conflicts arise, take a moment to calm down before addressing the issue. Use phrases like, "I

Daddy, Let Go of My Hand

forgive you," or "Let's work on this together," to reinforce a positive resolution.

Building strong roots and bonds with young children requires dedication, love, and intentional effort. It is about showing up every day, not just physically, but emotionally and spiritually. It is about creating a safe space where they can grow into their fullest potential, knowing they are loved and supported. As a parent, you have the profound privilege of shaping their world and leaving a legacy of love that will carry them through life. By being a "daddy" in every sense of the word, you are not just raising a child, you are raising a resilient, compassionate, and confident human being.

Acknowledgments

I would like to take this opportunity to express my heartfelt gratitude to everyone who played a role in bringing this book to life.

First and foremost, my deepest thanks to my wife Edwina, children Zylo and Zander. Your unwavering support, patience, and encouragement have been the foundation of this journey. To my family and friends, thank you for believing in my vision even when the path seemed unclear.

To my editors, your keen eye and thoughtful insights have elevated this work to a level I could not have achieved alone. Thank you for your dedication and for pushing me to refine my ideas with care and precision.

Daddy, Let Go of My Hand

To my publisher and the entire team, your professionalism, expertise, and tireless efforts have turned this manuscript into the book it is today. Thank you for your guidance every step of the way.

To the beta readers and early supporters who took the time to provide feedback, I am eternally grateful. Your constructive criticism and kind words gave me the motivation to keep moving forward.

To the community of readers, writers, and creatives who have inspired me along the way, thank you for reminding me of the power of storytelling.

Lastly, to you, the reader: thank you for picking up this book and allowing it to become a part of your world. I hope it resonates with you in ways that are meaningful and lasting.

Charles Danso

With deepest gratitude,

Charles Danso.

The End.

Charles Danso